ALONG THE SHORE

DISCOVERING STARFISH

Lorijo Metz

PowerKiDS press.

New York

To Steve, who is a fish, and also a star in our eyes

Published in 2012 by The Rosen Publishing Group, Inc.
29 East 21st Street, New York, NY 10010

First Edition

Editor: Amelie von Zumbusch
Book Design: Kate Laczynski

Photo Credits: Cover, p. 10 iStockphoto/Thinkstock; p. 4 Art Wolfe/Getty Images; p. 5 Jupiterimages/Goodshoot/Thinkstock; p. 6 Brandon Cole/Visuals Unlimited, Inc./Getty Images; pp. 7, 9 (bottom), 11, 17, 20–21, 22 Shutterstock.com; p. 8 Jupiterimages/Photos.com/Thinkstock; p. 9 (top) © www.iStockphoto.com/lillisphotography; p. 12 Norbert Wu/Getty Images; p. 13 David Wrobel/Getty Images; p. 14 Stephen Frink/Getty Images; p. 15 (top) © www.iStockphoto.com/mlwinphoto; p. 15 (bottom) © www.iStockphoto.com/Nancy Nehring; p. 16 David Fleetham/Visuals Unlimited, Inc./Getty Images; pp. 18–19 © Jeffrey L. Rotman/Peter Arnold.

Library of Congress Cataloging-in-Publication Data

Metz, Lorijo.
    Discovering starfish / by Lorijo Metz. — 1st ed.
        p. cm. — (Along the shore)
    Includes index.
    ISBN 978-1-4488-4996-3 (library binding)
    1. Starfishes—Juvenile literature. I. Title.
    QL384.A8M48 2012
    593.9'3—dc22

                                                2011000152

Manufactured in the United States of America

CPSIA Compliance Information: Batch #WS11PK: For Further Information contact Rosen Publishing, New York, New York at 1-800-237-9932

CONTENTS

STARFISH

Starfish belong to the group of animals called **echinoderms**. Echinoderms were on Earth over 200 million years before the dinosaurs! They are some of the most common animals on Earth. However, echinoderms are found only in the ocean. Along with starfish, sea urchins, sea cucumbers, brittle stars, and sea lilies are all echinoderms.

These starfish are bat stars. They live along the shores of the Pacific Ocean from Alaska to Baja California.

This girl found a dried starfish on a beach. People sometimes take dried starfish home with them to remember their time along the shore.

There are five classes, or groups, of echinoderms. Starfish belong to a class called **Asteroidea**. This means "star-shaped." While most starfish do look like stars, none of them are fish. Fish have **backbones**. Echinoderms do not. For this reason, many people call starfish sea stars.

WHERE DO STARFISH LIVE?

Each **species**, or kind, of starfish has its own special **habitat**, or place to live, in the ocean. Some live in the icy waters of the Arctic Ocean. Others live in the warmer waters of the South Pacific. Some live deep in the ocean. Others live close to the shore.

These ochre sea stars are in a tide pool at Point of Arches, in Olympic National Park. This is along the Pacific coast in Washington.

This starfish lives in the Red Sea. The Red Sea is an arm of the Indian Ocean that separates Africa from Asia. Its water is warm and quite salty.

Some starfish float quietly through the water, while others stay put on sandy ocean floors.

One of the best places to see starfish is in a **tide pool**. Tide pools are pockets of water that form along rocky shores when the tide comes in. When the tide goes out, starfish stay wet by hiding under rocks and seaweed.

WHAT DO STARFISH LOOK LIKE?

Most starfish have five arms, called rays. Some have up to 40. Starfish rays grow around a **central disk** in the middle of their bodies. A hard, shell-like skin gives them shape. Starfish have tiny spots, called **eyespots**, on the tips of their rays. Eyespots let starfish sense light and dark. Other parts of their skin help them sense smells.

This is a sunflower starfish. These starfish can be orange, yellow, red, brown, or purple. They grow to have many rays.

Ochre sea stars, such as these two found along the coast near Vancouver, British Columbia, have five rays.

Starfish have hundreds of tiny tube feet on the bottoms of their rays. They move using waterpower. Water comes in through openings in their central disks. The water flows through their bodies and is pushed out their tube feet.

You can see the tube feet on the bottom of this starfish's ray. Starfish move around and hold on to rocks and sand with their tube feet.

HOW AND WHAT DO STARFISH EAT?

Most starfish crawl along the ocean floor and eat when they sense food nearby. They are slow movers, and so are the animals they eat. Many starfish eat clams, oysters, and mussels. Some starfish eat seaweed. Others eat coral

This starfish is eating a mussel. You can see it holding on to the mussel with its tube feet.

This cushion sea star is about to eat a sea urchin. Cushion sea stars eat many foods. They often draw food out of the sand.

and sponges. Still others eat tiny pieces of food floating in the water or mixed in the mud.

Starfish have a strange way of eating shellfish. First, a starfish wraps itself around the shellfish. Next, it uses its tube feet to pull the shell apart. Then, it pushes one of its two stomachs out through its mouth and into the shell. The starfish's stomach breaks down the soft animal inside.

MAKING NEW STARFISH

Female starfish produce hundreds, or even millions, of eggs each year. Most females cast their eggs into the water. Only a few of the eggs survive to become **larvae**, or baby starfish. These soft, tiny creatures look nothing like their parents. Larvae eat tiny plants and animals. They

This *Diplasterias brucei* is brooding. These starfish are one of a few species that brood, or carry around and watch over their babies.

This northern sea star lost three of its five arms. However, as you can see, the missing arms are growing back.

go through many growth stages before becoming adults. Starfish also have another way to **reproduce**, or make more starfish. When starfish are struggling with their enemies, they may lose one of their rays. If enough of the central disk remains attached to the lost ray, it will grow into an entirely new starfish!

STARFISH FACT

Blue starfish are also called comet stars. A new starfish can grow out of a blue starfish's arm even if it does not have part of the central disk attached. Most other starfish cannot do this.

NORTH AMERICAN STARFISH

Many starfish live in North America. Ochre sea stars can be found in tide pools along the Pacific coast from Alaska to Mexico. These starfish are often purple but also can be orange or brown.

Forbes' sea stars live along the Atlantic coast from the Gulf of Maine to Texas. They are one of the most common starfish

STARFISH FACT

One of the most colorful starfish in North America is the blood star. Blood stars are best known for being bright red, but they can be many different colors.

This cushion sea star is in the waters off of Key Largo, Florida. These starfish live in the Atlantic Ocean. They are most common in the Caribbean Sea.

You can see several differently colored ochre sea stars in this picture of a tide pool in Washington's Olympic National Park.

there. In fact, they are also known as common starfish.

Sunflower starfish are huge. They can be more than 3 feet (1 m) wide. They live in deep waters from Alaska to Southern California. These starfish begin life with 5 rays and add more as they grow. They can have as many as 24 rays.

Bat stars live along North America's Pacific coast. They get their name because some people think that their wide rays look like bat wings.

There are about 1,800 species of starfish in the world. The smallest are paddle-spined sea stars. These starfish are smaller than a child's fingernail. They are found along the coast of Australia. To keep from being swept away by waves, they live in seaweed.

One of the heaviest starfish is the Catala's sea star. It can weigh as much as 13 pounds (6 kg).

Candy cane starfish live in the Indian Ocean and western Pacific Ocean. They are also called necklace sea stars, marble sea stars, and peppermint sea stars.

Granulated sea stars, such as this one, live in the Pacific Ocean and Indian Ocean. They are common on Australia's Great Barrier Reef.

These fat, white-and-pink starfish live in the Pacific Ocean near the Philippines, Indonesia, and Australia's Great Barrier Reef. This **coral reef** is built of the remains of tiny living things called corals. It is home to many animals, including several kinds of starfish.

STARFISH FACT

Starfish often look like their names. Chocolate chip starfish look like they have chocolate chips on them. Candy cane starfish are red and white, like candy canes!

STARFISH AND ECOSYSTEMS

A place and all of the things living in it make up an **ecosystem**. The plants and animals living in an ecosystem depend on one another. Starfish are an important part of many saltwater ecosystems.

Some northern sea stars live in tide pools along the Gulf of Maine. Plants and other animals, such as blue mussels, live there, too.

Northern sea stars eat blue mussels. Blue mussels help keep the water clean. However, they will quickly take over the places where they live. If northern sea stars did not eat blue mussels, they would take over the tide pools and push out the other things that live there.

Northern sea stars are important in many ecosystems along North America's Atlantic coast. These northern sea stars are feeding on a bed of mussels in the waters off of New England.

STARFISH AND PREDATORS

Starfish have hard, often prickly, skin. This makes them hard to eat. However, sea turtles, seagulls, and even other starfish eat them.

Giant Triton snails also eat starfish. They are one of the main predators of crown-of-thorns starfish. These animals live on coral reefs. Crown-of-thorns starfish eat coral. Giant

Crown-of-thorns starfish live in the Pacific Ocean and Indian Ocean. This crown-of-thorns starfish is feeding on coral in the Red Sea.

Tritons keep the numbers of these starfish under control by eating them.

People started collecting giant Tritons for their beautiful shells. Today, there are few left. With so few giant Tritons left, there are now many more crown-of-thorns starfish. This means more coral is getting eaten. This puts the reef and the animals that live there in danger.

STARFISH FACT

If a starfish loses a ray, it will grow another one. This comes in handy when fighting predators. Sometimes starfish give up a ray just to get away.

PEOPLE AND STARFISH

Surprisingly, not everyone likes starfish. Some people complain that starfish eat clams, oysters, and other animals people like to eat.

In general, though, people love collecting starfish. Their fun, starlike shape comes in equally

This purple starfish is an ochre sea star. Ochre sea stars are among the most common starfish in the Pacific Northwest.

fun colors. They are also easy to catch. You can often find starfish along beaches when the tide is low. Tide pools are another great place to find starfish. If you do not live near the beach, look for starfish at an aquarium.

GLOSSARY

Asteroidea (AS-teh-royd-ee-uh) The class, or group, of animals to which all starfish belong.

backbones (BAK-bohnz) Rows of bones in people's or animals' backs that hold up their skeletons.

central disk (SEN-trul DISK) The part in the middle of a starfish's body.

coral reef (KOR-ul REEF) An underwater hill of coral.

echinoderms (ih-KY-nuh-dermz) A group of sea animals with no backbones and tube feet.

ecosystem (EE-koh-sis-tem) A community of living things and the surroundings in which they live.

eyespots (EYE-spots) Spots on an animal that sense light.

habitat (HA-buh-tat) The surroundings where an animal or a plant naturally lives.

larvae (LAHR-vee) Animals in the early period of life in which they have a wormlike form.

reproduce (ree-pruh-DOOS) To make more of something.

species (SPEE-sheez) One kind of living thing. All people are one species.

tide pool (TYD POOL) An area of shallow water at the seashore that is surrounded by rock.

INDEX

WEB SITES

Due to the changing nature of Internet links, PowerKids Press has developed an online list of Web sites related to the subject of this book. This site is updated regularly. Please use this link to access the list:
www.powerkidslinks.com/alsh/starfish/